Medieval Gardens

Medieval Gardens

Anne Jennings

ENGLISH HERITAGE

IN ASSOCIATION WITH THE MUSEUM OF GARDEN HISTORY

Front cover: **A scene from the French manuscript** Des profits ruraux des champs *illumination, by Pietro di Crescenzi c1475–1500*

Back cover: **Chives,** Allium schoenoprasum

Published by English Heritage, 23 Savile Row, London W1S 2ET
in association with the Museum of Garden History, Lambeth Palace Road,
London SE1 7LB

Copyright © English Heritage and Museum of Garden History
Anne Jennings is hereby identified as the author of this work and asserts
her moral right to be recognised as the copyright holder in the text.

First published 2004

ISBN 1 85074 903 5

Product code 50922

A CIP catalogue for this book is available from the British Library

Edited and brought to press by Adèle Campbell
Designed by Michael McMann
Technical editor Rowan Blaik
Printed by Bath Press

Contents

Introduction

This book provides an introduction to our early gardens: how they were designed, maintained and enjoyed. Far from being a mere footnote to medieval life, gardens were as important in the Middle Ages as they are today. Most were sources of food and medicine, while others also provided a backdrop to courtly love and space for contemplation. The privileged man could have a garden created purely 'for the delight of…sight and smell'.

Detailed records made by monastic and lay communities provide a fascinating insight into the wide-ranging influences on these early gardens. Some manuscripts are directly concerned with gardening but there are more clues, captured in other documents ranging from the Domesday survey to individual household accounts. Many garden scenes are depicted in illuminated manuscripts, either as scenes of everyday life or as allegories of Paradise and romance. These varied sources give us a surprisingly detailed picture of gardens in the Middle Ages.

The book includes a number of practical 'how-to' sections giving tips on creating medieval-style features in your own garden. Lists of flowering plants, herbs and trees at the end of the book can provide ideas for planting that will evoke a medieval feel. The lists include the availability of the plants, as seeds and container-grown specimens, in UK nurseries.

A wild-flower planting scheme on the earthworks of Berkhamsted Castle, Hertfordshire

The evolution of medieval gardens

The medieval period was a time of unprecedented change in Britain, dominated by foreign influence that was to impact on British life for centuries to come. Romans had ruled for the previous 500 years, but with their departure in the 5th century Britain fell prey to successive Viking invasions and Anglo-Saxon England was dominated by rule from the north. These Dark Ages were brought to an end in 1066 when William, Duke of Normandy, defeated King Harold at the Battle of Hastings. The new Norman elite ruled with a strong hand and transformed the culture of William's new kingdom, introducing French language, art, architecture and, ultimately, gardens into England.

This northern European influence can be seen in many of England's magnificent cathedrals. Ely, Durham, Lincoln, Winchester and Salisbury were built from the 11th century and Oxford and Cambridge Universities were established soon after. Rapid developments were made in medicine, mathematics and technology, including the production of paper, which was to have such an enormous impact on society. By the 15th century the Renaissance influences of mainland Europe had reached Britain and art, literature, music and learning blossomed. With the link to mainland Europe established, people and ideas arrived from more distant Mediterranean countries and those even farther afield, like Persia (now Iran), Turkey and Moorish North Africa.

A fruit picker from Pietro di Crescenzi's Opus Ruralium Commodorum

As a more sophisticated culture developed in England it was only a matter of time before gardens were created and appreciated for their beauty. While the Romans had introduced ornamental gardening to Britain during their occupation, it had virtually disappeared after their withdrawal. Life throughout the Dark Ages was harsh for most people and plants were cultivated out of necessity, to provide food and medicine. Gardening in this time of poverty and conflict moved closer to its agricultural origins, and only simple crops like pulses, cabbages, leeks, onions and edible wild plants were grown. The collapse of the Roman Empire and the ravages of Nordic invasions have left little evidence of ornamental horticulture during this time.

Harvesting parsnips and carrots

Gardens became an increasingly important aspect of medieval life and, as well as producing plants used for food and medicine, they were ultimately appreciated as places of leisure. As interest in gardens developed, so the need for skilled gardeners increased. Monks had long been expert horticulturalists as, even through the Dark Ages, they grew a wide range of plants within the safe enclosures of monastery walls. For the first time, however, professional gardeners were appointed to manorial households where they were held in high regard, as well-educated, highly skilled professionals who took on administrative as well as horticultural responsibilities. Gardeners were often given titles that described the most important facet of their work, for example, 'Keeper of the Vines'. But gardening was not the preserve of the aristocracy and the monasteries. The decline of feudalism in the 13th century created a new class of yeomen and farmers: labourers who leased their own land and lived in their own houses, around which they made small, productive gardens.

Preparing the vines, detail from an Italian fresco

5

Monastic gardens

The gardening carried out in monasteries throughout the Dark Ages was highly influential in the development of ornamental medieval gardens. The monks passed on plants and skills to their secular neighbours and have left detailed records that are invaluable to today's garden historians.

Monastic communities were self-sufficient and the monks were experienced in gardening, farming and medicine. Monks were educated and literate, and the detailed records they kept provide us with a wealth of information about their daily lives, including the management of their gardens. The monasteries would typically have several areas of 'garden' serving different functions. The kitchen garden would provide fruit and vegetables for the monks' table, and is often referred to as the *leac-garth* after the leeks that were such staple produce. Larger monasteries would have vineries and orchards. Fruiting trees would either have been adapted native varieties or grafts from European monasteries; among those favoured by the monks were medlar, mulberry and quince.

Early monastic orchards were planted in rows or patterns like the quincunx (with five objects arranged so that four are at the corners of a square or rectangle and the fifth at its centre). This method would have allowed maximum air and light to reach the trees but no doubt the layout would also have been appreciated

'...Where the peach-tree turns its leaves this way and that In and out of the sun...'

Mulberry, Morus nigra

for its beauty. Close to the infirmary would have been a herb garden, providing medicinal plants and herbs. A typical garden arrangement is shown on the plan of the 9th-century St Gall's monastery in Switzerland. This shows separate vegetable and physic, or medicinal, gardens as well as an 'orchard cemetery' where fruit trees were planted among the tombs.

The garden had rectangular, edged beds, laid out in a formal sequence and narrow enough for the monks to cultivate them from the surrounding paths, to avoid treading on and compacting the soil. Marked as 'paradise' on the plan is a garden area to which the outside community was not admitted, a private garden for quite contemplation that was also a flower garden, blooms from which would be used to decorate the church.

The monks introduced the practice of 'strewing' – spreading plants across the floor to form an aromatic carpet that disguised bad smells and helped ward off diseases and bugs. Plants were also used to dye fabric and their flowers, full of symbolic meaning, would decorate the church and be tied into tussie mussies (posies), nosegays and pomanders to hold near the nose when offensive smells were at their worst. These practices were adopted by rich and poor alike as knowledge spread from the monasteries to the wider population, and even continue to the present day: strewing is practised every Rush Sunday (Whitsunday) at the church of St Mary Redcliffe in Bristol, when the Alderman and Lord Mayor of Bristol carry nosegays and process down the main aisle which is scattered with herbs and rushes.

The rush-strewn aisle of St Mary Redcliffe, Bristol

Monastic records are not restricted to factual information, and more poetic descriptions conjure vivid images of beautiful gardens that clearly gave pleasure to the monks and local people. Poet and monk Walahfried wrote *De Cultura Hortulorum* in the 10th century:

> ....*I can picture you sitting there in the green*
> *enclosure of your garden*
> *Under apples which hang in the shade of lofty*
> *foliage,*
> *Where the peach-tree turns its leaves this way*
> *and that*
> *In and out of the sun, and the boys at play,*
> *Your happy band of pupils, gather for you*
> *Fruit white with tender down and stretch*
> *Their hands to grasp the huge apples....*

Translation by Payne 1966

The Norman invasion allowed commercial and religious links to develop between England and mainland Europe and new monastic orders with roots in Italy and France were established. These brought international influence to monastic gardens and plants, seeds, and horticultural and medicinal knowledge were exchanged between British and European monasteries. The southern European herbs, Southernwood,

Artemesia abrotanum and hyssop, *Hyssopus officinalis*, are examples of plants that are thought to have arrived in British monasteries around this time. Royal, military and commercial travellers also brought plants and seeds back to England, as well as images and inspiration for garden designs and layout, so that Europe, Turkey, Persia, the Holy Land and Arab countries all influenced early British gardens.

Common houseleek, Sempervivum tectorum

make a tussie mussie or nosegay

A tussie mussie or nosegay is a collection of flowers and herbs, tied together to form a small bunch. In the Middle Ages they were held up to the nose to ward off infection and create a sweetly scented barrier against offensive smells. The Queen carries a nosegay at the Maundy ceremony, although this is made in the larger, Victorian style.

The simplest tussie mussie can be made using a random selection of herbs and flowers like those suggested in the list below. A few of the suggestions were introduced in the Tudor period, so you can avoid these if you wish to stay closer to a true medieval posy.

- Choose unblemished material with perfectly formed flowers and leaves. Cut stems to roughly 6 inches (150mm) long,

- Carefully remove any lower leaves that would be squashed when the bunch is tied.

- Hold the cuttings together tightly and secure them with a rubber band, then cover with a decorative, waterproof ribbon.

Keep your tussie mussie fresh in a glass or small pottery vase filled with water.

If you feel more adventurous have a go at making a more formal tussie mussie:

- Choose an eye-catching flower for the centre such as the striped Rosa Mundi, *Rosa gallica* 'versicolor'.

- Surround this with a ring of grey cotton lavender, *Santolina chamaecyparissus*, then build up concentric rings of other herbs.

- Place five smaller flowers evenly around the outside of the final ring of herbs. A pink (*Dianthus*) or 'Love-in-a-mist', *Nigella damascena,* would work well.

- To give some structure, create an outer ring of something with a more woody stem, such as rosemary, *Rosmarinus officinalis* or cotton lavender

- Secure with a rubber band covered with a decorative, waterproof ribbon.

Try making seasonal tussie mussies, using forget-me-not, primrose and violet in spring and evergreen plants like yew and box with rosehips in autumn. A culinary tussie mussie can be made from bay, thyme, sage and other herbs mixed with edible flowers like nasturtium and chives.

**Ideal plants for yo
tussie mussie:**

Box
Campion
Columbine
Corncockle
Cotton lavender (Tu
Feverfew
Germander
Hyssop
Lavender
Love-in-a-mist (Tudo
Marjoram / oregano
Pink
Pot marigold
Primrose
Roses
Rosemary
Sage
St John's wort
Thyme
Violet
Wallflower

Monastic records are incredibly valuable to garden historians but there are a variety of other sources of information that can tell us, albeit indirectly, what medieval gardens looked like, how they were used and what was grown in them.

One early and illuminating documentary source is part of a Latin/Saxon dictionary: *The Glossary to Grammatica Latino-Saxonica,* written by Aelfric, Abbot of Eynsham, in 995. Included in Aelfric's vocabulary are around two hundred plants, herbs and vegetables, both native and Roman introductions, that were in general use at the end of the first millennium. The same document gives us the Saxon term *luffendlic stede,* meaning 'lovely place' and the Saxon word for garden: *wyrttun.*

Documents such as legal decrees and account rolls contain important information about medieval society and how people lived. The *Domesday Book* of 1086, commissioned by William I to discover who owned land and how it was being used, records almost 40 vineyards that had probably survived from Roman times, showing that a certain amount of sophisticated horticulture did continue through the Dark Ages. Monastic gardens were crucial to the continuation and development of gardening in Britain and it is enlightening to discover from *Domesday* that the monks in Worcestershire

'*...so that men may sit down there to take their repose pleasurably when their senses need refreshment.*'

owned more than a dozen valuable manors with large gardens. Account rolls not only detail purchases made by medieval gardeners, such as young plants and pots, but also tell us the gardeners' wages; a 13th-century gardener in the Bishop of Winchester's new garden at Rimpton in Somerset, for example, earned 1 shilling for grafting fruit trees. Property deeds are useful too: by the 14th century these show a clear difference between functional kitchen gardens and the 'pleasaunce' or pleasure garden.

French poetry and prose, Flemish and Belgian illuminated manuscripts, woodcuts and embroidered tapestries all tell us a great deal about these early gardens. Though there is little direct evidence for British gardens, links with mainland Europe were strong and our gardens would have shared many features with those in other European countries.

Medieval illustrations are often symbolic, using idealised plants and garden layouts to portray the hidden meaning of a poem or story. *Le Roman de la Rose* is a mid-12th-century poetic story about a lover who dreams of a garden and imagines himself falling in love with a beautiful maiden, symbolised by a rosebud. Later in the poem he is seduced by Lady Idleness in a walled garden that represents the Garden of Eden. This popular poem of over 22,000 lines was written by two poets over a period of 40 years, and was the inspiration for many

Many of the characteristic elements of medieval gardens feature in this illustration to Le Roman de la Rose

illustrations of medieval gardens. This section has been translated as prose but provides a clear image of the wooded area of garden:

> …quinces and peaches, nuts, chestnuts, apples
> and pears, medlars, white and black plums, fresh,
> rosy cherries, service-berries, sorb-apples, and
> hazel-nuts…great branching elms, together with
> hornbeams and beeches, straight hazels, aspens
> and ash trees, maples, tall firs, and oaks…spaced
> just as they should be, more than ten or twelve
> yards separating one from another, and yet the
> branches were long and high and so dense up
> above in order to protect the place from heat,
> that the sun could never penetrate to the earth
> and damage the tender grass.

Common medlar, Mespilus germanica

The writings of observers and diarists of the time provide a more literal record of medieval gardens. Albertus Magnus visited the homes and gardens of the great and wealthy as he travelled throughout Europe in the 13th century, as described in his *De Vegetabilibus et Plantis* in 1260:

> [About the lawn may be] planted every sweet-
> smelling herb such as rue, and sage and basil,
> and likewise all sorts of flowers, as the violet,

columbine, lily, rose, iris and the like. So that
between these herbs and the turf, at the edge of
the lawn set square, let there be a higher bench
of turf flowering and lovely; and somewhere in
the middle provide seats so that men may sit
down there to take their repose pleasurably
when their senses need refreshment.

Translation by John Harvey

A 15th-century 'Garden of Paradise'

Other educated medieval writers adopted a more scientific approach to understanding nature. Another 13th-century writer, Bartholomew de Granville, produced a series of encyclopaedias one of which was devoted to plants. He described the difference between plants and animals:

For trees move not wilfully from place to place
as beasts do;
neither change appetite and liking, nor feel
sorrow…

In the mid-12th century a plan was made of the water supply to Christ Church Canterbury, Kent; commonly referred to as

Ox-eye daisy, Leucanthemum vulgare

The 13th-century plan of Canterbury Cathedral: the herber is to the south of the church

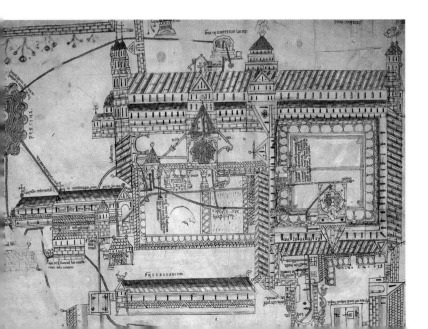

the 'waterworks drawing', the plan also shows the cathedral priory's herb garden. Garden archaeology has also contributed a great deal to our knowledge of medieval gardening practices. Excavations have revealed evidence for features such as fishponds, viewing points and enclosures, as well as for the lay-out of beds. Fragments of ornamental plant pots have been uncovered and it is even possible to detect which plants were grown, by identifying plant remains that have been preserved through burning, waterlogging or drying. Excavations at Mount Grace Priory in Yorkshire have added to our knowledge of the practices of the hermit-like order of Carthusian monks who lived there in the 14th century, revealing that each monk had his own garden attached to his living quarters or cell.

Mount Grace Priory, North Yorkshire, and a reconstruction of a monk's cell and garden

This wealth of sources has inspired some authentic reproductions of medieval gardens, such as the one created by Sylvia Landsberg in Winchester in the 1980s. It is in the style of a small enclosed garden, or herber, and is named for two queens: Eleanor of Provence, wife of Henry III, and the Spanish garden-loving queen of Edward I: Eleanor of Castile. Eleanor of Castile is known to have brought gardeners to England from Spain, and when not in the royal palace of Leeds Castle in Kent, she stayed at Winchester with her husband. Sylvia Landsberg took inspiration and ideas from illuminated manuscripts and details on surviving local buildings of the period. The garden is planted authentically with herbs, roses and simple flowering plants like hollyhocks (thought to have been brought to England from the Holy Land by Eleanor of Castile) and pot marigolds, and is a fine demonstration of how garden historians can recreate period gardens by interpreting a variety of information.

Within the walled enclosure is a grassy bower, a tunnel arbour, fountain and pool, and a herber, or secluded sitting area. During the medieval period certain plants were symbolically associated with particular religious or personal virtues, and among the plants present in Queen Eleanor's Garden, holly, ivy and bay represent the medieval ideal of faithfulness. Roses, columbine and strawberry plants all represent various aspects of Christian spiritual philosophy.

build woven hazel enclosures

Woven hurdles or fence panels are very popular today and can be bought direct from craftsmen or from specialist suppliers who often advertise in the classified section of gardening magazines. Ready-made panels are sold in a range of sizes and are usually supplied in hazel, *Corylus avellana*, although willow is also available.

The wood from which the hurdles are made has been coppiced. This involves cutting down all the growth to a stump every seven or eight years, then harvesting the resulting new growth, or poles, prior to the next coppicing. It is a traditional craft that was practised long before the Middle Ages, and it has played an important part in the development and character of our ancient woodlands and forests. The young, flexible poles are put to a variety of commercial uses today, not only for hurdles but also for walking sticks, broom handles, furniture and wooden rakes.

The ready-made panels can be used to make an instant woven hazel enclosure to give a medieval feel to your garden.

First consider how high you want the boundary to be; do you want total privacy and seclusion or would rather look out onto the surrounding area? Next decide on the size of the area you want to enclose. Check the manufacturer's details for the widths of hurdles they supply, then calculate how many hurdles, and of which height, you will need for the area you want to enclose.

Both ends of every hurdle must be fixed to a stout timber post, which should be concreted into the ground. Your local garden centre or builder's merchant can advise you on the best way to do this. If your panels are high, or if your garden is on an exposed site, it is advisable to use posts that are 8 feet (2.4m) high and about 3 inches (80mm) square. Sink 2 feet (600mm) of the post into the earth leaving 6 feet (1.8m) above ground. For lower panels, or on a sheltered site, you can simply use round tree stakes hammered into soft earth, making sure at least 1 foot (300mm) is below ground so the posts remain stable.

Once the posts are firmly in place, you need to fix the panels in place with nails or tied them with galvanised wire (which is protected against rust); again your garden centre can advise on the best materials to use.

The hurdles will create an attractive backdrop to your medieval garden and you can train climbing plants up them which, when established, will provide extra interest. Climbing roses, honeysuckle, hops or ivy are all ideal.

Centres that specialise in the continuation of rural crafts, such as the Weald and Downland Museum in Sussex, often run courses on hazel weaving. With a little extra knowledge and practice you would be able to make your own hurdles and more ambitious features such as covered seats, pergolas and plant supports.

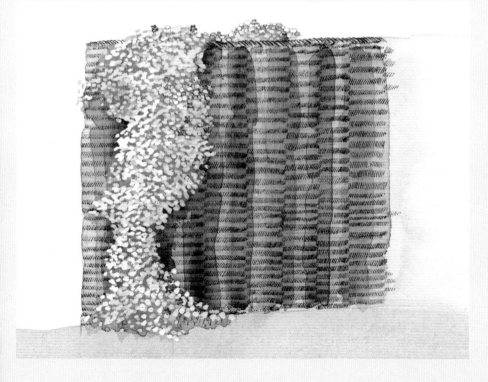

'Jon the Gardener', who was thought to have worked in one of the English royal gardens around 1400, detailed the horticultural practice of the time in a poem. Here he describes how to graft vines.

> *Clean atwain the stock of the tree*
> *Wherein that they graft shall be.*
> *Make thy cutting of the graft*
> *Between the new and the old staff*
> *So that it be made to lie*
> *As the back and the edge of a knife.*
> *A wedge thou set in midst the tree*
> *That every side from other flee*
> *Till it be opened wide*
> *Wherein the graft shall be laid.*

Our techniques for fruit training have hardly changed since Roman times

Poems like Jon the Gardener's, together with other written and illustrative records, tell us a great deal about medieval garden craft. Techniques introduced by the Romans for training fruit and ornamental trees, and for other forms of propagation, continued to be used. These practices not only applied to ornamental horticulture but were also used commercially in vineyards and tree nurseries.

Several medieval images illustrate gardeners at work and show that the tools they used have remained almost

Hollyhock, Alcea rosea

unchanged over the centuries. The range of wooden and iron spades, rakes and forks are recognisable, and wheelbarrows were used too but appear to have been cumbersome and difficult to manoeuvre. An impressive range of cutting tools was at the disposal of the medieval gardener: pruning knives, billhooks, axes, saws, sickles, scythes and shears were all available. Ladders were used for collecting top fruit, which was placed into bags and baskets worn around the body.

Illustrations also show that wicker baskets were used as plant containers, and documents suggest that ceramic pots were also common, which is supported by archaeological finds of ornamental plant holders from medieval gardens. Tender plants would be lifted at the first sign of frost, replanted in pots and kept under cover, just as they are today. Young trees and fragile plants were supported by simple woven frames.

A town garden with woven plant supports and edged lawns

Left: **Pruning and grafting in the 13th century**

Opposite: **15th-century gardeners at work**

While continental influence played a part in developing the gardens of the wealthy, the poor looked closer to home for inspiration for their plots. Monasteries were often open to the local community who would go there to worship or perhaps to receive help or medicine from the monks, and the peasants copied the formal, geometric layouts and narrow rectangular beds, similar to those used in ornamental vegetable gardens today. Peasants' gardens were small, fenced areas attached to their dwellings, on which they grew pulses, cabbages, leeks, onions and edible wild plants such as pot marigold, *Calendula officinalis*. The gardens were utilitarian, but the vegetables were interspersed with essential but pretty wild flowers; a combination that was to be seen centuries later in the cottage style of gardening.

'...the lord and the lady may dwell, when they wish to escape from wearisome occupations...'

Opposite: **Pot marigold, Calendula officinalis**

Peasant gardens in a Bohemian fresco of c1400

A yeoman's garden of the late medieval period has been recreated at the Weald and Downland Museum in West Sussex. The Bayleaf Farmhouse is a more substantial dwelling than a peasant's cottage, befitting a man of the emerging agricultural middle class, and is surrounded by a small but well-managed plot of land. Within this, the enclosed kitchen garden is laid out with rectangular vegetable beds divided by simple paths. Herbs and medicinal plants are grown in separate beds that are slightly removed from the vegetable garden.

While the poor were tending their small plots the rich were busy moulding their outdoor spaces simply for fun and relaxation. Hunting, riding, jousting and other sports like archery took place within safely enclosed areas, and festivities and celebrations took place in the 'tamed' forests that were by that time under royal ownership. These pleasure parks extended out from the castle into the wider landscape and were enclosed by expensive brick walls. Some, such as Henry II's Woodstock, extended over several miles. They were planted with trees and shrubs to provide a habitat for deer, rabbits and hares, while a summerhouse would provide a place for relaxation. Larger parks had rivers or ponds as well as aviaries and menageries, all to provide an experience of the vast outdoors without endangering the lords and ladies of the court. The delights of the pleasure park were described in detail by Pietro di Crescenzi in 1305, in *Opus Ruralium Commodorum*:

The Bayleaf Farmhouse, Weald and Downland Museum

*Opposite: **A high-status garden, with elegant fencing, a brick-faced seat and ornate plant containers***

… inasmuch as wealthy persons can by their riches and power obtain such things as please them and need only science and art to create all they desire. For them therefore, let a great meadow be chosen, arranged and ordered … it should be twenty 'Journaux' or more in size according to the will of the Lord and it should be enclosed by lofty walls. Let there be in some part a wood of diverse trees where the wild beasts find a refuge. In another part let there be a costly pavilion where the king and his queen or the lord and the lady may dwell, when they wish to escape from wearisome occupations and where they may solace themselves…

Britain was warmer in the 13th century than it is today and these safe gardens, whether herbers or parks, provided the ideal environment for outdoor entertainment; for dining, playing music and, importantly, for courtly romance. From purely practical beginnings, 13th-century writers reveal a growing appreciation of the aesthetic qualities of plants and flowers. In *De Vegetabilibus et Plantis*, for example, Albertus Magnus writes in 1260:

> *There are however, some places of no great*
> *utility or fruitfulness…these are what are called*
> *pleasure gardens. They are in fact mainly*
> *designed for the delight of the two senses, viz*
> *sight and smell.*

The need to enclose gardens continued through the 12th century; to protect those inside from wild animals but also as defence against the Anglo-Saxons who continued to revolt against Norman rule. Rich and poor alike used coppiced timber to build their boundaries in the form of fences and trelliswork, and native trees such as willow and hazel were cut to provide long flexible rods that were woven or tied into decorative hurdles. The peasant's boundary was rustic and coarse but the wealthy refined their timber structures to create decorative features, screens and plant supports. In the late medieval period more substantial, decorative wooden

Ladies at work in a 15th-century garden

pillars were used and the very wealthy built brick and stone walls. Laid hedges and hedgerows formed living boundaries and those who could afford to often refined their planted screen to incorporate topiary and other plant training techniques, with climbing plants tied into timber screens.

Within the boundary the garden was usually laid out in a formal design, with a square central lawn dissected by paths and surrounded by borders. A fine lawn was as coveted in medieval gardens as it is today and appreciation of the green sward extended beyond the aesthetic:

> The green turf which is in the middle of the material cloister refreshes encloistered eyes and their [the monks'] desire to study returns. It is truly the nature of the colour green that it nourishes the eye and preserves the vision.

Hugh of Fouilloy c1132–1152

The ground was thoroughly levelled and all weeds were removed before meadow turf was laid. This was kept as a tight, low-growing carpet by expert scything and weeds and moss were regularly removed. Small wild flowers like daisy, Bellis perennis, speedwell, Veronica officinalis and thyme, Thymus praecox subsp. Brittanicus, were sometimes introduced into the turf to create a flowery mead, and the effect is described well by 14th-century writer Giovanni Boccaccio in *The Decameron*:

> *In the midst of the garden a lawn of very fine grass, so green it seemed nearly black, coloured with perhaps a thousand kinds of flowers…shut in with very green citrus and orange trees bearing at the same time both ripe fruit and young fruit and flowers so that they pleased the sense of smell as well as charmed the eye with shade.*

Bejewelling the lawns in a walled town garden

Another version of the flowery mead, with taller plants cultivated in the turf, is illustrated in some 15th-century paintings and embroideries and sometimes referred to as the 'bejewelled lawn'. However, it is hard to know how true a representation of medieval gardens these provide, as the artists often depicted plants that flower at different times of the year: for example primroses, spring snowdrops, iris and roses blooming together. It is difficult to imagine how such a planting scheme would have been successfully maintained.

Snakeshead fritillary, Fritillaria meleagris

create a flowery mead or bejewelled lawn

A simple flowery mead can be created by allowing low-growing plants like daisies and cowslips to establish on an existing lawn. This will often happen if a lawn is not cut for a few weeks, but you can introduce them by scattering seeds or planting young plants in the form of 'plugs'.

At certain times of year a flowery mead or 'bejewelled lawn' could be one of the most attractive features in your medieval garden, though maintaining the balance between grasses, ornamental flowers and pernicious weeds can be time-consuming. Plantains, dock, moss and creeping buttercup can quickly take over large sections of lawn so remove young plants as they appear.

The following principles apply equally to new or established lawns. Experiment with a small area first – a raised bed would be ideal. In a larger garden you could try separate spring- and summer-flowering lawns. Once you have the idea you can experiment with different plants – you might not always be successful but it will be fun to have a go.

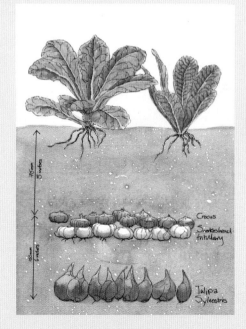

A spring flowering mead – plant in late autumn

Select a range of small, spring-flowering bulbs, for example snakeshead fritillary, *Fritillaria meleagris*, and the naturalised wild tulip *Tulipa sylvestris*. Push these into the soil before you lay turf, or through established turf – you can buy a special tool for this from garden centres or cut out small sections with a trowel if necessary. Once the bulbs are in place, carefully plant young cowslips and primroses through the turf.

The bulbs will eventually push their noses through the grass and you will have a lovely display of flowers from early to late spring. After flowering, allow the foliage to turn yellow before cutting or pulling the leaves away. In a small area the grass can be trimmed with shears, taking care around the primroses and cowslips. The following spring the plants will all flower again and you will gradually find they increase through division and self-seeding.

A summer flowering mead – sow in spring

This will work best on a sunny, sheltered site. You will need a mixture of hardy annual seeds, such as flax and pot marigold. Sprinkle the seeds, mixed

with fine sand to aid even distribution, onto the soil or grass using a garden sieve. If sowing a new area, add a fine quality grass seed (choose bents or fescues) to the mix, gently cover the seeded area with a fine layer of soil and lightly water. Proportions will vary according to the conditions of the site but in general use 4g of wild-flower seed per square metre (⅛ oz to 1 square yard) and 25–30g grass mix per square metre (¾ oz to 1 square yard)

You may need to cover the area with garden net and twigs to prevent interference from birds and cats. Keep the soil moist while the seeds are germinating, and as the grass and flowers emerge keep an eye out for any unwanted plants that may have self-sown – groundsel or dandelions for example – and remove them immediately.

In summer you will have a delicate and colourful display of flowers intermingled with long grass. Allow seedheads to dry and drop their seeds before carefully cutting all the growth back with shears, or a mower for larger areas. The flower seeds should germinate the following spring when the cycle will begin again, but you can add more seed if necessary.

A summer flowering 'bejewelled' lawn – plant in spring

Choose a selection of summer-flowering perennials in small pots, for example lychnis and campion, and container-grown bulbs including lilies and rhizomes such as iris. Plant these through the turf.

This lawn will demand more attention through the flowering season as the turf should be clipped short around the plants. If you want to try this in a larger area, position the plants in well spaced groups so that it is possible to manoeuvre a small mower around them.

At the end of the flowering season you should cut the top growth back, but leave healthy iris leaves on the plants.

While the lawn was an open, sunny place, some shade was also desirable. Productive trees planted in and around the edge of the grass, either as individual specimens or as part of an avenue, would create pleasant dappled shade, ensuring comfort from the sun and protection for fair skin.

> Upon the lawn, too, against the heat of the sun, trees should be planted or vines trained, so that the lawn may have a delightful and cooling shade, sheltered by their leaves. For from these trees shade is more sought after than fruit, so that not much trouble should be taken to dig about to manure them, for this might cause great damage to the turf. Care should also be taken that the trees are not too close together or too numerous, for cutting off the breeze may do harm to health…let them be sweet trees, with perfumed flowers and agreeable shade, like grape-vines, pears, pomegranates, sweet bay trees, cypresses and such like.'

De Vegetabilibus et Plantis by Albertus Magnus 1260

More shade was provided by arbours and pergolas created from supple poles of hazel or willow arched across rough timber supports. Pergolas could be open-sided but often had

French manuscript illumination of c1470, Emilia weaves a garland in a herber

square grid trellis panels in the side sections, providing a framework for trained plants. The trellis often incorporated 'windows' to view the wider landscape from the safety of the enclosure. Wealthier men commissioned more elegant wooden structures that were planed and jointed like the one in Queen Eleanor's Garden.

Timber, stone or turf seats provided places for relaxation and contemplation under the shade, as well as for more frivolous pursuits like singing and courting. Contemporary illustrations of medieval secular gardens show seats of raised turf banks with sloping or straight sides, retained by wattle hurdles or a brick wall and planted with low-growing species like daisies, speedwell and, later in the period, camomile, *Chamaemelum nobile*. These seats were sometimes arranged in a U-shape or 'exedra' which could accommodate a trestle table for diners

or be used as a backrest by someone sitting on the ground. Different designs provided intimate nooks for private conversations or allowed enough space for dancing. Large wooden benches were sometimes placed around the garden for full reclining and sleeping.

A mixture of flowers and herbs was planted in raised beds and borders around the lawn; a system that demonstrates good horticultural practice as many plants benefit from improved drainage and deeper root runs when they are grown in raised beds. The beds were edged with low woven hurdles, timber, tiles or even cleaned animal bones set with the knuckle joint facing upwards to create an ornamental effect.

Dancers from Le Roman de la Rose

Paths ran between borders, beneath pergolas and around and across the lawn. The materials used varied according to the formality of the garden and the wealth of its owner. At their simplest the soil was scraped away until a firm stone or flint subsoil was reached, and the excess earth could be piled up to create the raised beds. Turf, gravel or sand (or a mixture of the two) would be used where a refined effect was desired. Local stone was also used but bricks were very expensive and rarely used.

Pools, fountains and channels, or rills, also featured in medieval gardens. Illustrations of European examples suggest a strong Persian influence, featuring fountains of stone, bronze and lead elaborately decorated with lion heads, falcons and crowns. It is likely that British water features were somewhat simpler, perhaps created by diverting a stream or spring to fill pools linked by rills. *Le Roman de la Rose* gives us an idea of the effect:

Sir Robert Vaughan's recreated medieval garden at Tretower Court, Powys

Here and there were bright springs, free from insects and frogs and shaded by the trees, but I cannot say how many. Little streams ran in channels constructed by Pleasure, and the water made a sweet and pleasant sound

Guillaume de Lorris 1237 and Jean de Meun 1277
(Translation by Chaucer)

Water forms a boundary on one side of this walled garden

Water also served a surprising variety of practical purposes, with pools maintaining a regular supply of fish for the kitchen or providing water to dampen a falcon's wings before flight.

build a raised turf seat and flower bed

A raised seat and flowerbed can be built from bricks but an easier and cheaper method is to use timber railway sleepers. It is now illegal (and inadvisable) to use second-hand railway sleepers for garden furniture and other domestic purposes, because they are impregnated with harmful tar and creosote, but the new softwood sleepers that you can buy instead are lighter and easier to handle. The sleepers are usually 8'6" long, 9" wide and 5" deep (2.4m x 250mm x 125mm). You must find a safe way of cutting them; your supplier or other local timber merchant should cut them to size for you but if not you should find someone who is qualified to use a chain saw.

As new sleepers are usually pale in colour you might want to stain them, though you can let them weather naturally. You could also face the structure with low woven hurdles or split hazel poles to give it a more authentic look.

Decide how long and wide you want your seat to be. If you intend to face it with woven hurdles you may want to work to the size of hurdle supplied by the manufacturers. Aim to make your seat roughly 18" (450mm) high, bearing in mind that the base will need to be sunk roughly 2 inches (50mm) into the ground. The sleepers should be staggered as they are laid to provide greater stability, and you will need to take this into account when calculating the number of sleepers you need and the length to cut them to. If you want a narrower edge around the top of the structure you can replace the top level of sleepers with sawn and treated timber, 5" (250mm) square.

Make sure the ground is level and the earth well compacted before you begin. Set the bottom row of sleepers roughly 2 inches into the ground, and build up the layers in a staggered pattern so the joints do not sit directly above each other. Fix each sleeper in place with a 6" (150mm) galvanised nail, hammered diagonally down into

the one below. Secure any narrower timber around the top of the seat with 8" (200mm) countersunk screws, and fill the hole above the screw with an outdoor quality wood filler.

Fill the seat to roughly 12 inches (300mm) below the surface with fine grade builder's rubble and make sure it is well compacted. If you tell your

supplier the dimensions of the area you need to fill they will work out you how much you need. The rest of the seat should be filled with topsoil from a reputable supplier, who can guarantee it is clean and free from perennial weeds. Again the supplier will calculate the amount you need, but as it settles over the next few weeks you might find you need to top it up.

Tread the topsoil down firmly as you go along, until it is level with the top of the timber. Leave it to settle for as long as you can – if you can build your raised bed in autumn and leave it through winter before planting this would be ideal. Before planting, top up the soil and tread it firmly once more. At this point you can nail low hurdles to the front and sides of the seat if you wish. A good alternative would be split hazel poles from a coppicing project, which you can nail horizontally onto the sleepers; you might need to drill holes prior to nailing to avoid splitting the hazel.

If your seat is in full sun plant it with a creeping thyme or camomile; the camomile variety 'Trenague' is ideal, as it doesn't flower but forms a dense mat of foliage. In shadier areas creeping mint should thrive, or use fine grade turf. The latter can be sown as seed, but if you prefer to lay turves remember your soil level needs to be approximately ⅗ inch (15mm) below the timber. Sweet woodruff will do well in part shade or sun.

For the surrounding flower bed use a mixture of low-growing and taller plants. Herbs such as catmint, marjoram, chives, woodruff and houseleeks are good for a sunny spot, while mints, wood sage, parsley and borage are a better choice for shadier areas. Taller plants can include lavender, rosemary and hyssop and should be planted at the ends where they won't interfere with the seating area.

Wild marjoram, Origanum vulgare

Symbolism was important in medieval gardens and was derived from pagan and Islamic religion as well as Christian beliefs. Rich and poor alike attributed spiritual significance to nature but in different ways; peasant tradition focused on plants and celebrated the change of seasons, whilst wealthier members of society appreciated symbolic interpretations of both natural and man-made garden features.

On a simple level, the rites and traditions celebrated by the poor reflected their dependence on nature to meet their basic human needs. With the comforts most of us enjoy today it is hard to appreciate the full impact of the arrival of spring in a time when cold, dark winters would have confined people to the unhygienic and pungent indoors. As the days lengthened people could move around outdoors in comfort once again, and the new season's plants and flowers would provide them with fresh food, as well as colour and scent to make life more pleasant.

Hawthorn, Crataegus monogyna

Spring was a time for celebration and plants played an important part in the revelry. Garlands of flowers, wreaths and crowns, flower 'dressing' of graves and wells and the Easter celebrations were times of great excitement. May saw the height of fertility celebrations when flowers were used to decorate maids and their lovers as well as those pagan symbols of fertility, maypoles. In their earliest form these had vines or thin twigs knotted together to form long leafy strands in place of the ribbons used today. The May Queen was traditionally given a crown of hawthorn, *Crataegus monogyna*, as part of a fertility rite that pre-dates Christianity.

A wealthy family's garden in the 14th century might have been influenced by the Islamic design ideas that were reaching England from Spain. Islamic gardens incorporated classic geometry into their design, with streams or canals leading to a central feature. Water held religious and mystical significance associated with its cleansing properties and was also perceived to be a source of life. Where running water formed a cross, its four sections represented the quarters of the universe; three merging streams of water might refer to ancient Persian culture or to the Christian concept of the Trinity, three in one. The enclosed garden, the *hortus conclusus*, often symbolised the Old Testament's Garden of Eden, and in Christian belief the garden itself represented Christ and the church, bearing 'fruits of the spirit'.

In Britain it is likely that Islamic influences were gradually translated to reflect Christian beliefs. Plants often represented the Virgin Mary's qualities: the rose was considered her special flower and the violet represented her humility. Mary's purity was seen in *Lilium candidum*, known then as the White lily and later as the Madonna lily.

Medieval gardens served as a romantic backdrop to courtly romance, an essential feature of life in a world where arranged marriages meant love had to be acted out, perhaps in the hope that the real thing would follow. This courtly love in the garden is a main theme of the poetry and prose of the time and one of the most valuable sources of information is again *Le Roman de la Rose*, with its rich imagery and detailed illustrations.

This complex use of symbolism and the desire to integrate a deeper meaning into the design and layout of gardens suggests a sophisticated expectation of these outdoor spaces and how they were enjoyed, raising them above mere providers of aesthetic pleasure. An overriding desire to create 'paradise' seems to have underpinned the need to make beautiful gardens, perhaps understandable at a time when life was short and frequently brutal. The wealthy desired a foretaste of what was to come in the afterlife. As the medieval period drew to a close Britain absorbed influence from Renaissance Europe, and the interpretation and significance of gardens became more refined, challenging educated visitors to resolve puzzles and find hidden meanings.

*Opposite top: **Bathing maidens, from a Persian miniature***

*Opposite bottom: **Paradise depicted as a walled garden in the 14th-century** Holkham Bible Picture Book*

The picture shows the white lily, Lilium candidum: a symbol of purity that became known as the Madonna Lily

Plants

The 17th century saw the true beginning of a professional approach to plant hunting, but 'new' plants from foreign countries were already seducing wealthy gardeners and landowners in the Middle Ages. The Romans had brought many non-native plants to the country and while some survived after their departure, others were re-introduced at a later period. The quintessentially English common box, *Buxus sempervirens*, is a fine example. As early as the 11th century, travellers of many kinds were bringing home, by accident or design, plants and seeds from far afield. The common wallflower, *Cheiranthus cheiri* (now known as *Erysimum cheiri*) probably arrived in England with the Normans, its seed lodged among imported building stone. The pink or border carnation *Dianthus caryophyllus* may have travelled this route too, and still flourishes at Rochester Castle in Kent and among the spectacular ruins of Fountains Abbey, North Yorkshire.

Throughout history plants have illustrated the divide between rich and poor. While the rich could buy new introductions and exotic specimens, for the poor the process was rather more random. The native and common plants they traditionally grew occasionally gave rise to natural variants, expanding the range they cultivated. 'Exclusive' plants could perhaps be acquired from seeds or cuttings from the gardens of wealthy employers or landlords and over a period of years a specimen that was previously rare would become more widely grown.

'...they pleased the sense of smell as well as charmed the eye with shade.'

Clary, Salvia sclarea

While the poor cultivated basic vegetables like colewort (kale) for the pot and took their pleasure in whatever simple wild flowers grew nearby, the rich consumed luxurious fruits including quince, peaches and grapes, and enjoyed the exquisite blooms of roses and lilies.

Flowers were generally 'simple' in form except where natural variants arose, for example those with double flowers or variegated leaves. Understanding of nature did not extend to seed formation and man-made hybrids would not be developed for at least another 300 years.

Enjoying the beauty and fragrance of the rose, from the late 14th-century Tacunium sanitatis in medicina

The mandrake, *Mandragora officianarum*, has been enshrined in folklore for many centuries. This unusual and very poisonous plant is mentioned in the book of Genesis in conjunction with the pregnancies of Jacob's wives Leah and Rachel and, perhaps because of this, had a reputation in the Middle Ages as an aphrodisiac and an aid to conception. It was known to be a narcotic by Roman herbalists, who used it to deaden pain, but seems to have been lost after the Romans left, before its reintroduction to Britain in the mid-14th century.

Collecting this useful plant, however, was fraught with difficulty. The unusually shaped – some thought human-shaped – tap root was believed to shriek so loudly when torn from the earth that it would kill anyone within earshot. Using a dog to extract the plant was one way round this.

Another belief was that mandrakes grew from flesh fallen from the gallows, and its reappearance in Britain around the time the plague struck probably did little to alleviate its sinister reputation. The mandrake isn't all bad, however: once won from the ground and placed over the mantle it was believed to bring good fortune to the household.

'Fructus mandragore' – *the mandrake – from* Tacunium sanitatis in medicina

The appreciation of gardens for their beauty was a relatively new phenomenon, but traditional uses of plants continued to form an essential part of daily life for rich and poor alike. Monasteries detailed specific uses in their beautiful hand-illustrated herbals, though it is often difficult to identify which plants are being referred to.

Carl Linnaeus (1707–78) developed the system of naming plants that is still in use today, but prior to this plants were identified by common names that varied from region to region. This makes identifying the plants from contemporary sources problematic; who would know, for example, that the 'Langbefe' in Jon the Gardner's poem was Viper's bugloss, *Echium vulgare*, or that 'Feltwort' was common mullein, *Verbascum thapsus*?

Opium poppy, Papaver somniferum

To add further confusion, the same or similar names were sometimes used for different plants. 'Dittany', for example, referred to *Origanum dictamnus*, a form of marjoram, and 'dittander', *Lepidium latifolium*, was a member of the cress family native to the east coast of England. More confusing still, the plant sometimes known as false or white dittany today is the ornamental perennial 'burning bush', *Dictamnus albus*. Such dilemmas highlight the debt we owe to academics, such as garden historian John Harvey, who have identified the plants listed in these early works.

Although the herbals included a complex mixture of folklore, myths and mystical beliefs, much of the information has a sound scientific basis. Some plants, like the opium poppy *Papaver somniferum*, from which opium is derived, still form the base of many drugs today and homeopaths continue to use them in their treatments.

A pharmacist and his assistant in the herb garden

Many ingredients used in medieval cures and potions could be found in the wild or in the gardens of even the poorest families, where remedies were passed down through the generations. Wild garlic was applied as an antiseptic and sage was used for coughs and colds as well as in treating menstruation and liver-related problems. 'Lungwort', *Pulmonaria officinalis*, grew in woodlands and its common name gives a clue to its effectiveness in treating bronchial disorders. Like many treatments it could be taken as a hot drink or eaten as part of a meal, though some remedies were applied as a poultice with substances like lard and honey used as a binding agent.

Rue, Ruta gravaeolens

As well as having medicinal and culinary applications, scented herbs and plants were used to ward off offensive smells from open sewers, animal waste and the like. In the mid-14th century, the strewing and burning of aromatic herbs and the carrying of fragrant nosegays were believed to ward off the plague. The recently introduced Mediterranean basil was placed on windowsills to deter flies, and rue, *Ruta gravaeolens*, was thought to kill fleas.

Pot-pourri made from the petals of lilies and roses and scented leaves of aromatic herbs like lavender would be placed around the house, worn about the body or fixed to hanging clothes. Pure white skin was considered beautiful and young maidens always made sure they sat or walked in the shade of a tunnel, arbour or tree, but a potion made from elderflowers could also enhance their pallor.

Plants of course formed an essential part of the diet, and flowers and herbs were also used to add taste and texture. Anything available was thrown into the poor man's pot, including herbs like thyme, hyssop, parsley and mint. Nettles were used to make soup and horseradish added a spicy flavour to a pottage. These plants often served a dual purpose as they also maintained and improved the family's health. Plants like feverfew, *Tanacetum parthenium*, herb Robert, *Geranium robertianum*, and plantain, *Plantago major*, are often considered weeds today but were an essential part of the ornamental and practical garden of the time. Plants such as pot marigold, *Calendula officinalis*, violet, *Viola odorata* and chive flowers, *Allium schoenoprasum*, also found their way onto the menu, so the recent fashion for using flower petals in salads in fact has its roots in medieval times.

Common elder, Sambucus nigra

Herb robert, Geranium robertianum, *colonising the ruins of Berkhamsted Castle, Hertfordshire*

'Messenger of the garden of souls'

Though it seems that the rose has always been the quintessential English flower, in fact most of its 150 or so species originated in Asia and the Persians dubbed the rose 'a messenger of the garden of souls'.

Britain's five native roses, or briars, would have been well known to both monks and lay people in the Middle Ages, but the garden roses we know today spring from different ancestors. One of these – *Rosa centifolio* 'Muscosa', the old Cabbage Rose – is said to be the most fragrant in the world, but it is *Rosa gallica*, the Apothecary's Rose and *Rosa alba*, the Great White Rose, that play a greater part in England's story.

The first English garden rose is thought to have been grown at Romsey Abbey in Hampshire, some time between the abbey's foundation in 967 and 1092, when William II is recorded as paying a visit to see the blooms (though more likely to see Edith, the young Saxon heiress who was staying there). The rose was seen as a symbol of purity and quickly developed associations with love, peace and paradise that endure to this day. In 1236 it also became a royal emblem, when Queen Eleanor of Provence brought the Great

Legendary symbols of feuding dynasties in Henry Payne's Choosing the red and white roses

White Rose with her on her marriage to Henry III. Eleanor's second son, Edmund, continued the royal connection when he became first Earl of Lancaster in 1275, and chose as his emblem the red Apothecary's Rose.

In later centuries these two roses became the distinctive badges of opposing royal dynasties – the red representing the house of Lancaster and the white the House of York – whose intermittent battles for the English throne were subsequently named the Wars of the Roses. Lancastrian Henry Tudor's victory over Richard III at the Battle of Bosworth Field in 1485 marks the end of the Middle Ages. The new king, Henry VII, married Elizabeth of York and marked their union, and that of the two royal houses, by combining the red and white roses into a new emblem. The Tudor rose has endured as the symbol of England for over half a millennium.

Plant lists

The following lists of plants, while not exhaustive, give an indication of plants that were available in medieval Britain. Only those of interest to the gardener have been included so crops like barley and wheat as well as 'non-ornamental' plants such as bracken and deadly nightshade are excluded.

All the plants listed are available in one form or another, whether as seed, container-grown plants or, in the case of some woodier plants, as bare rooted trees and shrubs.

If you want to plant a reproduction medieval garden you might find that some of the plants are not readily available in their simple forms. Often a plant like Yarrow, *Achillea millefolium*, will be available in garden centres as a range of modern hybrids. It is crucial then to decide whether your planting must be authentic or whether it is to be 'in the style of' medieval planting, in which case you will have a wider palette to select from and will find the plants easier to obtain.

Many cultivated forms of plants are only available as container-grown specimens because they are often propagated vegetatively, for example as cuttings or by layering. However, most annuals and many British wild flowers, native or naturalised, are rarely sold in garden centres as established plants because they are short-lived and uneconomical to grow on a commercial scale. Your only option for acquiring such plants will be to grow them from seed obtained from specialist suppliers. If you buy wild-flower seeds as part of a 'wild-flower mix', make sure you are happy wth the ratios.

Please remember that under the Wildlife and Countryside Act it is illegal to uproot any wild plant and to take material from protected species. All the plants listed in this book are available from legitimate sources.

The naturalised wild tulip, Tulipa sylvestris

Flowering plants and ferns

BOTANICAL NAME	COMMON NAME	PLANTS	SEED
Acanthus mollis	Bear's breech	🪴🪴	◈
Achillea millefolium	Common yarrow	🪴	◈ ◈
Achillea ptarmica	Sneezewort	🪴	◈
Adonis aestivalis	Summer adonis	🪴	◈ ◈
Agrimonia eupatoria	Common agrimony	🪴	◈
Agrostemma githago	Corn cockle	🪴	◈
Ajuga reptans	Bugle	🪴	◈
Alcea rosea	Hollyhock	🪴	◈
Alkanna tinctoria	Alkanet	🪴	◈
Althaea officinalis	Marsh mallow	🪴	◈ ◈
Anchusa officinalis	Alkanet	🪴🪴	◈ ◈
Anthriscus sylvestris	Cow parsley	🪴🪴	◈ ◈
Aquilegia vulgaris	Common columbine/ Granny's bonnet	🪴	◈ ◈
Arctium lappa	Greater burdock	🪴	◈
Arum maculatum	Lords and ladies	🪴	◈
Asplenium scolopendrium	Hart's tongue fern	🪴🪴	◈
Bellis perennis	Daisy	🪴	◈
Berberis vulgaris	Common barberry	🪴	◈
Bryonia dioica	White bryony	🪴	◈
Calamintha sylvatica	Wood calamint	🪴	◈
Calendula officinalis	Common marigold	🪴	◈ ◈
Centaurea cyanus	Cornflower	🪴	◈ ◈
Convallaria majalis	Lily of the Valley	🪴🪴	◈
Crataegus monogyna	Common hawthorn	🪴	◈

BOTANICAL NAME	COMMON NAME	PLANTS	SEED
Crocus sativus	Saffron crocus	🌱	🗂
Cynara cardunculus Scolymus Group	Globe artichoke	🌱 🌱	🗂
Delphinium staphisagria	Stavesacre	🌱	🗂
Dianthus caryophyllus	Border carnation/pink	🌱	🗂
Digitalis purpurea	Common foxglove	🌱	🗂 🗂
Digitalis purpurea f. albiflora	White flowered foxglove	🌱 🌱	🗂
Echium vulgare	Viper's bugloss	🌱	🗂
Eryngium maritimum	Sea eryngo/sea holly	🌱	🗂
Erysimum cheiri syn Cheiranthus cheiri	Common wallflower	🌱	🗂 🗂
Euphorbia amygdaloides	Wood spurge	🌱	🗂
Filipendula ulmaria	Meadow sweet	🌱 🌱	🗂 🗂
Fragaria vesca	Wild strawberry	🌱	🗂
Fritillaria meleagris	Snake's head fritillary	🌱 🌱	🗂
Galanthus nivalis	Common snowdrop	🌱	🗂
Genista tinctoria	Dyer's greenweed	🌱	🗂
Geranium robertianum	Herb robert	🌱	🗂

Common yarrow, Achillea millefolium

BOTANICAL NAME	COMMON NAME	PLANTS	SEED
Geum urbanum	Herb bennet	🪴	📦
Hedera helix	Common ivy	🪴	📦
Helleborus niger	Christmas rose	🪴 🪴	📦
Helleborus orientalis	Lenten rose	🪴	📦
Hesperis matronalis	Dame's violet/sweet rocket	🪴 🪴	📦 📦
Hyacinthoides non-scripta	Bluebell	🪴	📦
Hyoscyamus niger	Henbane	🪴	📦
Hypericum androsaemum	Tutsan	🪴	📦
Hypericum perforatum	Perforate St John's wort	🪴	📦 📦
Inula helenium	Elecampane	🪴 🪴	📦

Rose campion, Lychnis coronaria

BOTANICAL NAME	COMMON NAME	PLANTS	SEED
Iris 'Florentina'	Florentine iris		
Iris germanica	Bearded iris		
Iris pseudacorus	Yellow iris		
Knautia arvensis	Field scabious		
Lamium album	White deadnettle		
Lamium maculatum	Spotted deadnettle		
Lilium candidum	Madonna lily		
Lilium pyrenaicum	Yellow Turk's cap lily		
Linum perenne	Blue flax		
Linum usitatissimum	Common flax		
Lunaria annua	Honesty		
Lupinus albus	White lupin		
Lychnis coronaria	Rose campion		
Lychnis flos-cuculi	Ragged robin		
Lythrum salicaria	Purple loosestrife		
Malva sylvestris	Common mallow		
Mandragora officinarum	Common mandrake		
Narcissus pseudonarcissus	Wild daffodil		
Nigella sativa	Black cumin		
Paeonia mascula	Coral peony		
Paeonia officinalis	Common peony		
Papaver rhoeas	Common poppy		
Papaver somniferum	Opium poppy		
Pimpinella anisum	Aniseed		

BOTANICAL NAME	COMMON NAME	PLANTS	SEED
Plantago major 'Rosularis'	Rose plantain	🪴	◈
Polygonatum multiflorum	Common solomon's seal	🪴	◈
Polypodium vulgare	Common polypody	🪴 🪴	◈
Potentilla reptans	Creeping cinquefoil	🪴	◈
Primula veris	Common cowslip	🪴 🪴	◈ ◈
Primula vulgaris	Primrose	🪴 🪴	◈ ◈
Pulmonaria officinalis	Common lungwort	🪴	◈
Ranunculus acris	Meadow buttercup	🪴	◈
Rhamnus cathartica	Purging buckthorn	🪴	◈

Soapwort, Saponaria officinalis

BOTANICAL NAME	COMMON NAME	PLANTS	SEED
Rosa x alba 'Alba Semiplena'	White Rose of York		
Rosa gallica var. officinalis	Apothecary's rose		
Rosa moschata	Musk rose		
Rubia tinctorum	Dyer's madder		
Ruscus aculeatus	Butcher's broom		
Salvia sclarea	Clary		
Saponaria officinalis	Soapwort		
Sedum anglicum	English stonecrop		
Sedum telephium	Orpine		
Sempervivum tectorum	Common houseleek		
Silene latifolia	White campion		
Silene dioica	Red campion		
Smyrnium olusatrum	Alexanders		
Stachys officinalis	Betony		
Tanacetum parthenium	Feverfew		
Tanacetum vulgare	Tansy		
Teucrium chamaedrys	Wall germander		
Valeriana officinalis	Common valerian		
Verbascum thapsus	Great mullein/feltwort		
Veronica chamaedrys	Germander speedwell		
Vinca minor	Lesser periwinkle		
Viola odorata	Sweet violet		
Viscum album	Mistletoe	seed-borne parasite, grows on other plants	

Herbs

BOTANICAL NAME	COMMON NAME	PLANTS	SEED
Allium schoenoprasum	Chives		
Allium ursinum	Ramsons		
Anethum graveolens	Dill		
Anthriscus cerefolium	Chervil		
Artemisia absinthium	Absinthe		
Artemisia vulgaris	Mugwort		
Borago officinalis	Borage		
Carum carvi	Caraway		
Chamaemelum nobile	Chamomile		
Cichorium intybus	Chicory		
Coriandrum sativum	Coriander		
Cuminum cyminum	Cumin		
Foeniculum vulgare	Fennel		
Galium odoratum	Sweet woodruff		
Hyssopus officinalis	Hyssop		
Isatis tinctoria	Woad		
Lavandula angustifolia	English lavender		
Lavandula stoechas	French lavender		
Levisticum officinale	Lovage		
Melissa officinalis	Lemon balm		
Mentha pulegium	Pennyroyal		
Mentha spicata	Spearmint		
Nepeta cataria	Catmint		
Ocimum basilicum	Basil		

BOTANICAL NAME	COMMON NAME	PLANTS	SEED
Origanum majorana	Sweet marjoram	🌱	🌾 🌾
Origanum vulgare	Wild marjoram	🌱 🌱	🌾
Petroselinum crispum	Parsley	🌱	🌾 🌾
Rosmarinus officinalis	Rosemary	🌱 🌱	🌾 🌾
Rumex acetosa	Common sorrel	🌱	🌾 🌾
Ruta graveolens	Rue	🌱	🌾 🌾
Salvia officinalis	Common sage	🌱 🌱	🌾 🌾
Symphytum officinale	Common comfrey	🌱	🌾
Teucrium scorodonia	Wood germander	🌱	🌾
Thymus serpyllum	Wild thyme	🌱	🌾
Thymus vulgaris	Common thyme	🌱	🌾
Valeriana officinalis	Common valerian	🌱 🌱	🌾
Verbena officinalis	Common vervain	🌱	🌾

Wall germander, Teucrium chamaedrys

Top and soft fruit

BOTANICAL NAME	COMMON NAME	PLANTS	SEED
Corylus avellana	Hazel	🪴	🌱
Ficus carica	Fig	🪴	🌱
Fragaria vesca	Wild strawberry	🪴	🌱
Humulus lupulus	Common hop	🪴	🌱
Juglans regia	Common walnut	🪴 🪴	🌱
Malus domestica	Apple	🪴 🪴	🌱
Malus sylvestris	Crab apple	🪴	🌱
Mespilus germanica	Common medlar	🪴	🌱
Morus nigra	Black mulberry	🪴 🪴	🌱
Prunus avium	Wild cherry	🪴	🌱
Prunus cerasus 'Morello'	Morello cherry	🪴	🌱
Prunus domestica	Plum	🪴 🪴	🌱
Prunus dulcis	Almond	🪴	🌱
Prunus persica	Peach	🪴 🪴	🌱
Punica granatum	Pomegranate	🪴	🌱
Pyrus communis	Wild pear	🪴	🌱
Ribes uva-crispa	Gooseberry	🪴 🪴	🌱
Rubus fruticosus	Blackberry	🪴 🪴	🌱
Vitis vinifera	Grape vine	🪴	🌱

Trees, shrubs and climbers

BOTANICAL NAME	COMMON NAME	PLANTS	SEED
Acer campestre	Field maple	🪴 🪴	◈
Alnus glutinosa	Common alder	🪴	◈
Betula pendula	Silver birch	🪴 🪴	◈
Buxus sempervirens	Common box	🪴 🪴	◈
Castanea sativa	Sweet chestnut	🪴 🪴	◈
Crataegus monogyna	Common hawthorn	🪴	◈
Cupressus sempervirens	Mediterranean cypress	🪴	◈
Cydonia oblonga	Quince	🪴	◈
Daphne laureola	Spurge laurel	🪴	◈
Fagus sylvatica	Common beech	🪴 🪴	◈
Fraxinus excelsior	Common ash	🪴	◈
Ilex aquifolium	Common holly	🪴 🪴	◈
Juniperus communis	Common juniper	🪴	◈
Lathyrus latifolius	Broad-leaved everlasting pea	🪴	◈ ◈
Laurus nobilis	Bay tree	🪴 🪴	◈
Lonicera periclymenum	Woodbine/honeysuckle	🪴	◈
Picea abies	Norway spruce	🪴	◈
Pinus sylvestris	Scots pine	🪴 🪴	◈
Platanus orientalis	Oriental plane	🪴	◈
Populus tremula	Aspen	🪴	◈
Prunus dulcis	Almond	🪴	◈
Quercus robur	Common oak	🪴 🪴	◈
Salix purpurea	Purple osier	🪴	◈
Sambucus nigra	Common elder	🪴	◈

BOTANICAL NAME	COMMON NAME	PLANTS	SEED
Sorbus domestica	Service tree		
Taxus baccata	Common yew		
Ulex europaeus	Gorse		
Viburnum opulus	Guelder rose		

Oak, Quercus robur

Vegetables

BOTANICAL NAME	COMMON NAME	PLANTS	SEED
Allium cepa	Onions / shallot	✿✿	▪▪
Allium fistulosum	Welsh onion	✿	▪
Allium ampeloprasum	Wild leek	✿	▪▪
Armoracia rusticana	Horse radish	✿	▪▪
Asparagus officinalis	Asparagus	✿	▪▪
Atriplex hortensis	Orach/red spinach	✿	▪
Beta vulgaris	Common beet	✿	▪▪
Brassica oleracea	Cabbage	✿	▪▪
Brassica rapa	Turnip	✿	▪▪
Cichorium endivia	Endive	✿	▪▪
Citrullus lanatus	Watermelon	✿	▪▪
Crambe maritima	Sea kale	✿✿	▪▪
Cucumis sativus	Cucumber	✿	▪▪
Daucus carota	Carrot	✿	▪▪
Lactuca sativa	Lettuce	✿	▪▪
Lens culinaris	Lentil	✿	▪
Lepidium sativum	Garden cress	✿	▪
Pastinaca sativa	Parsnip	✿	▪▪
Phaseolus vulgaris	Kidney bean	✿	▪
Pisum sativum	Pea	✿	▪▪
Raphanus sativus	Radish	✿	▪▪
Rorippa nasturtium-aquaticum	Watercress	✿	▪▪
Sium sisarum	Skirret	✿	▪
Spinacia oleracea	Spinach	✿	▪▪
Vicia faba	Broad bean	✿	▪▪

This modern cabbage, Brassica oleracea, *has a less leafy heart than its medieval ancestor*

Scoring system

Unusual = Not listed for sale in the RHS *Plant Finder* or *The Seed Search*

Available = available from up to 29 listed nurseries

Widely available = available from over 30 listed nurseries

Further reading

Batey, Mavis and Lambert, David *The English Garden Tour*. London: John Murray, 1990

Campbell-Culver, Maggie *The Origin of Plants*. London: Headline Book Publishing, 2001

Fearnley-Whittingstall, Jane *The Garden, An English Love Affair*. London: Weidenfeld & Nicholson, 2003

Harvey, John *Mediaeval Gardens*. London: Batsford, 1981

Hobhouse, Penelope *Plants in Garden History*. London: Pavilion, 1997

Innes, Miranda and Perry, Clay *Medieval Flowers*. London: Kyle Cathie, 2002

Landsberg, Sylvia *The Medieval Garden*. London: British Museum Press, 1996

Maby, Richard *Flora Britannica*. London: Chatto & Windus, 1997

McLean, Theresa *Medieval English Gardens*. London: Barrie & Jenkins, 1989

Royal Horticultural Society *RHS A–Z Encyclopaedia of Garden Plants* (Vols I & II). London: Dorling Kindersley, 2003

Strong, Roy *Gardens Through the Ages (1420–1940): Original Designs for Recreating Classic Gardens*. London: Cowan Octopus, 2000

— *Small Period Gardens: A Practical Guide to Design and Planting*. London: Cowan Octopus, 1992

The RHS Plant Finder

Published annually by the Royal Horticultural Society, the *Plant Finder* lists more than 65,000 plants available from 800 nurseries as well as contact details, maps and opening hours for all the nurseries listed. There is also an online version of the *Plant Finder* on the RHS website: www.rhs.org.uk

The Seed Search

Now in its 5th edition, *The Seed Search* lists over 40,000 seeds available from 500 seed suppliers, with details of where to find them. It also includes 9,000 vegetable cultivars. Compiled and edited by Karen Platt, and available online at: www.seedsearch.demon.co.uk

Fennel, Foeniculum vulgare

Useful organisations

The Museum of Garden History

The Museum of Garden History exists to enhance understanding and appreciation of the history and development of gardens and gardening in the U.K., and was the world's first museum dedicated to this subject. Its attractions include a recreated17th-century knot garden with historically authentic planting and collections of tools and gardening ephemera, as well as a well-stocked library.

www.museumgardenhistory.org

The Royal Horticultural Society

The RHS is the world's leading horticultural organisation and the UK's leading gardening charity dedicated to advancing horticulture and promoting good gardening. It offers free horticultural advice and a seed service for its members and has plant centres at its four flagship gardens.

www.rhs.org.uk

The Garden History Society

The Garden History Society aims to promote the study of the history of gardening, landscape gardens and horticulture, and to promote the protection and conservation of historic parks, gardens and designed landscapes and advise on their restoration. The Society runs a series of lectures, tours and events throughout the year.

www.gardenhistorysociety.org

The National Council for the Conservation of Plants and Gardens

The NCCPG seeks to conserve, document, promote and make available Britain and Ireland's garden plants for the benefit of horticulture, education and science. Its National Plant Collection scheme has 630 National Collections held in trust by private owners, specialist growers, arboreta, colleges, universities and botanic gardens.

www.nccpg.com

The Henry Doubleday Research Association

HDRA is a registered charity, and Europe's largest organic membership organisation. It is dedicated to researching and promoting organic gardening, farming and food. The HDRA's Heritage Seed Library saves hundreds of old and unusual vegetable varieties for posterity, also distributing them to its members. The HDRA currently manages the kitchen garden at Audley End, Essex, for English Heritage and runs Yalding Organic Gardens (see Places to visit).

www.hdra.org.uk

Centre for Organic Seed Information

Funded by DEFRA and run by the National Institute of Agricultural Botany and the Soil Association, the Centre for Organic Seed Information is a 'one-stop shop' for sourcing certified-organic seed from listed suppliers. It covers fruits, vegetables, grasses, herbs and ornamental plants among others.

www.cosi.org.uk

Places to visit

Bede's World Herb Garden
Church Bank
Jarrow
Tyne & Wear NE32 3DY
Tel: 0191 489 2106
E-mail: visitor.info@bedesworld.co.uk
www.bedesworld.co.uk

Bolton Castle
near Leyburn
North Yorks DL8 4ET
Tel: 01969 623981
E-mail: info@boltoncastle.co.uk
www.boltoncastle.co.uk

Geffrye Museum
Kingsland Road
London E2 8EA
Tel: 020 7739 9893
E-mail: info@geffrye-museum.org.uk
www.geffrye-museum.org.uk

The Herb Society Garden
Sulgrave Manor
Sulgrave
Banbury
Oxfordshire OX17 2SD
Tel: 01295 768899
E-mail: email@herbsociety.org.uk
www.herbsociety.org.uk

Iden Croft Herbs
Frittenden Road
Staplehurst
Kent TN12 0DH
Tel: 01580 891432
www.herbs-uk.com

Leeds Castle
Maidstone
Kent ME17 1PL
Tel: 01622 765400
E-mail: enquiries@leeds-castle.com
www.leeds-castle.com

Little Moreton Hall
Congleton
Cheshire CW12 4SD
Tel: 01260 272018
E-mail: littlemoretonhall
@nationaltrust.org.uk
www.nationaltrust.org.uk

Lyddington Bede House
Blue Coat Lane
Lyddington
Leicestershire LE15 9LZ
Tel: 01572 822438
E-mail: customers@english-heritage.org.uk
www.english-heritage.org.uk

Mount Grace Priory
Osmotherley
Northallerton
North Yorkshire DL6 3JG
Tel: 01609 883494
E-mail: customers@english-heritage.org.uk
www.english-heritage.org.uk

Prebendal Manor House
Church Street
Nassington
Northamptonshire PE8 6QG
Tel: 01780 782575
info@prebendal-manor.demon.co.uk
www.prebendal-manor.demon.co.uk

Queen Eleanor's Garden
Great Hall
The Castle
Winchester
Hampshire
Tel: 01962 846476
E-mail: info.centres@hants.gov.uk
www.hants.gov.uk

Sir Roger Vaughan's Garden
Tretower Court
Tretower
Crickhowell
Powys NP8 2RF
Tel: 01874 730279
E-mail: cadw@wales.gsi.gov.uk
www.cadw.wales.gov.uk

St Mary Redcliffe
Parish Office: 12 Colston Parade
Redcliffe
Bristol BS1 6RA
Tel: 0117 929 1487
E-mail: parishoffice
@stmaryredcliffe.co.uk
www.stmaryredcliffe.co.uk

Stockwood Park Gardens
Stockwood Park Craft Museum
Farley Hill
Luton
Bedfordshire LU1 4BH
Tel: 01582 546739
E-mail: museum.gallery@luton.gov.uk
www.lutonline.gov.uk

Weald & Downland Open Air Museum
Singleton
Chichester
West Sussex PO18
Tel: 01243 811363
E-mail: office@wealddown.co.uk
www.wealddown.co.uk

Yalding Organic Gardens
Benover Road
Yalding
Kent ME18 6EX
Tel: 01622 814650
E-mail: enquiries@hdra.org.uk
www.hdra.org.uk

Acknowledgements and picture credits

English Heritage and the Museum of Garden History would like to thank the many individuals who contributed to this volume, in particular Rowan Blaik for technical editing and James O Davies for photography, as well as colleagues at the National Monuments Record and Elaine Willis for picture research. Thanks to Royal Botanic Gardens Kew for allowing access to the gardens for photography and to Livvy Gullen for further research.

The author would like to acknowledge the invaluable assistance of Jane Wilson and Fiona Hope at the Museum of Garden History and Jan Greenland of the Herb Society for guidance on tussie mussies.

Unless otherwise stated, images are © English Heritage. English Heritage photographs were taken by James O Davies, except: facing p1 and p59, Nigel Corrie; p19l, Skyscan Balloon Photography. Reconstruction of Mount Grace Priory, p19r, by Claire Thorne. Original artwork by Judith Dobie.

Other illustrations reproduced by kind permission of:

AKG images: fc (Brit Lib MS Add.19720 f1,17v), 31, 32 (Brit Lib MS Add. 20698), 35 (Brit Lib MS Add. 19720 f.165), 41, 42, 50t (Brit Lib MS Or 12208, f.220), 50b (Brit Lib MS Add. 47682 f.4), 51, 54, 55, 57 (Erich Lessing); The Art Archive: 5 (Palazzo Schifanoia Ferrara/Dagli Orti (A), 26 (Archaeological Museum Cividale Friuli/Dagli Orti), 29 (Torre Aquila Trento/Dagli Orti (A), 43 (V&A Museum/Graham Brandon), 49 (Eileen Tweedy), 59, 73 (British Museum); Bridgeman Art Library: 2 (Giraudon), 4 (Bibliotheque Municipale, Rouen), 17 (Stadelsches Kunstinstitut, Frankfurt-am-Main), 26 (Bibliotheque de L'Arsenal, Paris), 27 (Lauros/Giraudon), 45 (Brit Lib MS Add. 19720 f.214), 60; British Library: 15 (Harl MS 4425 f.12v); CADW: 44; Jacques Amand: 36, 62; Master and Fellows of Trinity College: 18 (MS R.17.i); St Mary Redcliffe: 9; Weald and Downland Open Air Museum: 30.

Every effort has been made to trace copyright holders and we apologise in advance for any unintentional omissions or errors, which we would be pleased to correct in any subsequent edition of the book.

Other titles in this series

Georgian Gardens

Edwardian Gardens